AHEAD of My TIME

THE COLLECTOR'S EDITION

Poetry by

BERNARD SNYDER

Palmetto Publishing Group, LLC
Charleston, SC

For information regarding special discounts or for bulk purchases, please contact Palmetto Publishing Group at Info@PalmettoPublishingGroup.com.

ISBN-13: 978-1-944313-36-4
ISBN-10: 1-944313-36-2

SPECIAL THANKS

*I would like to give thanks to God first and foremost.
Because he has allowed me to live my dream as an
author and inspire others while doing so.*

*Also, I would like to thank everyone in the military
(or retired) that has risked his or her life for this beautiful
country of America. Bravo to all of you.*

*And lastly, I would like to say thanks again to Mr. Virgil
Hudson and Mr. Rodney Craig Holmes for the many intelligent
conversations, the late-night laughs and allowing me a place
of serenity by which this book was completed.*

Thanks to all of you!

"STILL STANDING"

When I look at the road from which I came
and bridges I had to cross,
the mountains I was asked to climb
and rivers I swam across,
it doesn't seem likely
I would still be able to stand
Adversity kept me on my knees constantly
But it also made me who I am!

"NATURE"

Interacting with nature is priceless. The falling of a leaf shows us that nothing lasts forever. The shifting of the tide tells us everything will change at some point, the morning dew signifies each day should be viewed as a fresh start, and the most profound of them all is the rainbow, which shows us no matter how much it rains, there's always hope!

"AHEAD OF MY TIME"

Many, many years from now, when you and I are nothing
more than two old angels soaring amongst the clouds,
somewhere in America there will be a teacher or professor
rewarding passing grades to any of his students who could
identify for whom most of my poetry was written. Some will
misspell your name, others will try researching your middle
name only to discover it was never used. Meanwhile, you and
I will be sharing a glass of wine on Pluto or Neptune and
laughing about those times people rode around in cars instead
of spaceships, and how at one point, folks were using cell
phones to communicate with one another, not knowing their
neighbors on Mars could hear everything they were saying.
But more importantly, I will remember the very first time I
saw you. How striking! We spoke on occasions. I remember
telling you I thought you were the most beautiful woman on
the planet, and that I would see you the exact same way if
I saw you in another lifetime. You chuckled in disbelief and
thought I was out of my mind. At that moment, I decided I
would pray every day and night so that when you and I meet
again years later, you would realize I wasn't out of my mind,
just far ahead of my time. And I'm certain I would still see
you on that day as I did way back then!

"MOVING RIGHT ALONG"

One day I will look back and reflect, reminisce a bit, might even frown at those things that didn't go right. But I won't ponder too long, because I understand some things weren't meant to be. And because of those things, I am able to proceed without ever having to look back again!

"THE WAY TO LOVE"

The way to love someone is to first trust and believe in what you feel, learn to enjoy those precious moments while they exist, have a clear understanding that people and feelings do change over time. So try and cherish that person today in a way that, if the two of you were to grow apart, you would always have a reason to smile!

"THE TEASER"

When I look back
at all the missed chances
The wilted roses and numerous advances
(I realize)
Even if I'd place
The entire world in her palms
Made her the exclusive topic
In every one of my songs
(it wouldn't have mattered)
Because the fact remained
We weren't on the same page
I wanted us to become one
She felt I was trying to invade
So I would throw my hands in the air
Turn to walk away
But she would slowly reel me back in
Using provocative word-play
(she was good at it too)
She said something to me once
That stayed on my mind
She said she could make the sun rise
Twice before lunchtime,
I'm sure she was hypothetically speaking
Still I found it awfully impressive

So I kept sending more and more roses
To show I was intrigued by the message
(but the flowers would always come back)
So I finally came to my senses
Decided to 'throw in the towel'
I realized she was just a tease
That didn't care much about flowers
Nor was I her 'cup of tea'
Or the one she'd show off to her homies
I just happen to be the subject
She liked for entertainment purposes only!

"BEHIND THE SMILE"

I've always known she was taken
But something about her made me keep trying
I used to flatter her with sweet pleasantries knowing
She would read between the lines,
I use to start a conversation with her
Just to see her smile
A lot of times I made no sense at all
But she knew my intentions all the while,
I'm sure she knew exactly how I felt
As I reflect back on it now
But a beautiful smile of acknowledgement
Was all she'd ever allow,
I'm not sure which I adored most
Her beauty or her style
Or how would I react
if I knew the thinking behind her smile!

"IF I COULD WRITE…"

I would first glance over
My most treasured photograph
Gather my thoughts
Then jot down a few paragraphs
(to talk about this lady)
I might go into details
About why I treasure her picture
Write five or six lines
Describing her fabulous features
(or maybe not)
I might just dot my I's
Make sure my T's are crossed
Use metaphors in each phrase
To keep her other friends lost
Or then again I might just admit
Writing isn't my thing
I gave it a shot
But all birds can't sing
And even though I may have been awful
With this paper and pen
I still came out a winner
Because the lady in this picture is somewhere smiling!

"SAVANNAH"

It's hard to believe what is happening
Right before my very eyes
This place I consider home
Has become notorious for senseless killings
and drive-bys,
As I try to grasp the reasoning
For this sudden outrage in my own people
I realize holding all-night vigils in the community
always bring us closer
but the core of the problem is much deeper,
So I thought I might convey a message
that would ease the tension on both sides
but no one cares to hear about love any more
than they care about the innocent people that have lost lives!

"WHERE I STAND"

As I've gotten somewhat older, I don't do some of the things I once did. Nowadays I trust only a few. I can actually count my 'true friends' on one hand. I no longer tolerate folks that only wants a favor. I keep a small circle so I won't have to entertain fake 'squares'. I listen to everyone, but when it comes a point where an important decision has to be made, I make sure it's one I can live with. I don't have one single enemy. If you don't like me, that's your problem not mine. I've learned over time that everyone isn't going to like me for one reason or another. How people feel about me isn't nearly as important as how I feel about myself. I've chosen to live this way because it's less stressful. Also, I cannot worry about things I can't control. And lastly, I find living with a pure heart doesn't just make me feel good about myself, it allows me to genuinely enjoy love!

"BROKEN PIECES"

Sometimes we sort through the shattered pieces
With hopes of finding something still intact
Despite the excruciating pain we went through
We always find ourselves looking back,
Too often we allow our hearts to lead us
Hoping for a second chance
Putting our entire lives on 'hold'
When we should be trying to advance,
We get so 'caught up' thinking of the good times
That we forget how the bad times left us hurt and speechless
Losing sight that all we have left
are memories and broken pieces.

"LIFE"

I assess my life as if it were a rose.
Despite the many thorns, it's still beautiful.

"A LONELY ROSE"

Something must've happened over time
No one seem to ever ask for me
Maybe I've lost my significance
Or the world is going through a catastrophe,
Maybe people don't love anymore
Which would make me totally worthless
I may as well become extinct
Because I have no other means or purpose,
No one says 'I love you' as I do
Or put hearts together just for the hell of it
But if I no longer have the same effect
What I once stood for is now irrelevant,
I just wanted to make a difference
And keep a smile upon a face,
Believe that I meant a lot more
Than just another flower in a vase!

"IF I HAD WINGS"

If I had wings I would paint the sky the same color as your eyes. I would draw an image of your smile and place it in front of the moon, just so everyone on earth and beyond would have something more scintillating to look up to. I would then transform every single star in the universe into mid-size soda bottles, which would replicate your well-defined curves and picture-perfect physique. And lastly, I would get down on my knees and thank the almighty for creating you, because by doing so, he simultaneously provided the muse of a lifetime for me.

"YOUNG MEN"

I would like to take a moment to address an issue that's been going on for some time. This message is for my young audience mainly. I may or may not know you personally, and who I am isn't important. This is about you. Of late, we've been hearing about a lot of senseless killings between the police and our young men across the nation. Well, we cannot change anything that has happened, but we can take some precautionary measures so this won't happen to you. We now live in a society where you are being stereotyped simply because of the way you dress and the fact that you're hanging out late at night. In my eyes, that is your choice. However, the police may feel you're up to no good for those two simple reasons alone. My advice is, you may have to dress more professionally, and when or if an officer pulls you over at night for some oddly reason, please try and be as polite as possible. I'm not saying this is the answer to the problem, but it might prevent one from ever occurring. Again, none of us really know the intent or emotions of the people involved in the previous tragedies, but I hope this message is conveyed so that we, as a people wouldn't have to experience another sad killing. I'm not trying to save the world, just one or two young men at a time.

"PARDON ME"

Pardon me for having a clear understanding that while you were judging me, your house wasn't in the proper order. Pardon me for not allowing your perception of me to define what I would become. Pardon me for not listening while you listed the many things I couldn't achieve. Pardon me for having you believe I was illiterate simply because my Gullah accent was somewhat unorthodox. Pardon me for not thanking you enough, because while you could only see the worst in me, it prepared me for someone that would appreciate me at my best!

"THE RIGHT ONE"
(Ladies)

When the right person walks into your life, you will forget that you were once too afraid to love. This person will give you a sense of comfort you've never experienced in your entire lifetime. He will make you feel as if you're the most beautiful woman in the universe. He will remember most, if not all dates pertaining to you. He will stand by your side through adversity. He will listen as you tell the same stories you've told him numerous times, not because it's interesting, but because he simply likes being in your presence. This person will love you unconditionally. And the most telling evidence that he's the one will be, not only will you appreciate him, you will be willing to genuinely love him in return.

"SOMEHOW"

Somehow I still hear her voice
Wherever I go,
Strangely, I still smell her perfume
Whenever the wind blows
I find this rather peculiar
Because this happens every day
I would understand it a lot better
If she didn't live so far away.

"THE RED ROSE"

To have stumbled upon you is truly a blessing. Your beauty is comparable to that of an evening sunset, equally as pleasing to the eyes as music is to one's ears. If I only had two wishes left on earth, they would be to become the arm that holds you at night and be the vase that protects you for as long as you are alive. I would keep you nourished by every sense of the word, not only to provide you strength, but allow you to grow and understand what it means to enjoy living. See, I don't look at you as just another flower, I see you as 'the red rose', which in comparison to all the other flowers in the universe, you are by far the most beautiful!

"NO DOUBT"

Company is easy to find when you have a lot to offer.
The person that stands by your side when you've got
absolutely nothing, is the one you should trust with
everything when you start making progress.

"WILD FLOWER"

Much like the rose that grew from the cracks of concrete
I was also disregarded and walked over repeatedly
Some folks had even predicted that I would fail immensely
Because the odds weren't in my favor
And the cards were stacked against me
But I kept my belief
In the talent God had given me
Applauded the naysayers
For unknowingly giving me a burst of energy
Because if it had not been for them
And those negative comments I had to withstand
I'm not sure I would've been so driven
In becoming the blossoming wild flower that I am.

"IN THE SHADOWS"

I'm searching everywhere for a little sunshine
Because all of my days have been gloomy
I'm trying to forget about my past life
Because all it does is consumes me
I'm constantly burdened by skeletons
Overcome by the darkness
I prefer to live in solitude
Because there isn't anyone I'd trust my heart with
I would like to walk away from this misery
And never look back at this
But for now I'm still trapped in the shadows
with nothing but memories of unhappiness.

"MONEY AND MISERY"

I once believed my life would be much happier if I had lots of money and just as many friends. As time passed I realized I was happiest when I had less of both!

"OVERWHELMED"

We often travel a path of uncertainty
Unsure of what lies ahead
We find someone that really intrigues us
But our heart isn't quite prepared
so we contemplate back and forth
So afraid it could be a mistake
We'd like to know where the road may lead us
But we're overwhelmed with so little faith,
We look for signs that would give us some idea
But everything seem so vague
A part of us would like to at least try
The other part too afraid,
so we think it is best to just walk away
not ever knowing if the pieces fit
we were so overwhelmed by fear
we didn't even have the heart to take the risk.

"GET READY"

Prepare yourself for success.
That way, if opportunity and reward happens
simultaneously, you would be ready to handle them both!

"MY TWO CENTS"

In this lifetime, you won't ever be able to please everyone.
Not everyone is going to like you for one reason or another.
So try to find peace wherever you go and with the ones that
bring you joy. Avoid people with negative energy. Negative
energy has a way of drawing you in if you're not careful.
We are all on this earth for a limited time only. So try and be
as happy as you can for as long as you can with the ones that
make you happy!

"CONFESSIONS"

I've made some mistakes
Burnt a few bridges
Got played once or twice
By some vindictive witches (but that's okay)
I met a sly fox once
Dressed in sheep's clothing
She had very nice qualities
But she was way too controlling
It seems we were playing 'poker'
I saw the hand she was 'holding'
When she started 'trippin' and tried to 'raise me'
I packed my bags and kept rolling' (Hadn't seen her since)
I've lost my share of cash
Trying get-rich quick schemes
Playing five lucky numbers
I'd envisioned in a dream
only to find out hours later
Nothing was ever what they seem
Another drawing went right on by and those numbers
never came (but that was okay too)
I've even rolled the 'dice' a few times
Still lucky to be alive
I went searching for hot '10's'
But all I found was 'snake eyes'

And even though this may sound strange
I feel it was a blessing in disguise
Because I am a much wiser person today having
survived the gambles and wild rides!

"BELIEVE IN YOURSELF"

A lot of people will doubt your abilities. Some will even critique the path you chose to get to where you needed to go. Just make sure your determination outweigh the negativity.

"ONE DAY.."

I will have a house on the hills
With a three-car garage
A panoramic view
So I can write under the stars,
Finally start to enjoy life
And do things my way
Own two sport cars
And have a 'Bentley 'parked in the driveway,
One day I'll know exactly how it feels
To shop at fine gift shops along Beverly-Hills,
Experience what it's like to have lunch in Paris
Find someone I loved enough
To even talk marriage,
I plan to live happily
And provide my kids' needs
Live amongst movie stars
And famous celebrities
But in order for me
To keep this real and exciting
I would have to stay focused
And never stop writing.

"DEAR SANTA"

Material things I'd never ask of you
Because I can get them on my own
But I've got a friend that's fighting a battle
She can't win all alone
I will always stand in her corner
Because that's what true friends do
But I realize I can't be there always
So here's what I need from you,
For Christmas, I want you to take her a box of happiness
So that her heart remains warm and splendid
You can leave the gift-tag unsigned
I'm quite sure she'd know who sent it!

"THE PERFECT POEM"

I contemplated repeatedly
Before I started to write this
I wasn't sure I would get your attention
Or if my words would seem lifeless,
I look at your picture
Filled with beauty and brightness
My mind feels you're so distant
But my heart says 'I like this'
Metaphorically I'm just an eagle
Talons tied and flightless
But if I had you by my side
My life would not only be perfect
It would be priceless!

"I TOO HAD A DREAM"

I also had a dream
Though mine wasn't quite as long
I dreamt the 'rose' I am attracted to
Could actually be a thorn,
I awoke from this nightmare
Confused and somewhat blue
Because my rose could very well be innocent
But my dreams have always come true.

"OMG"

Sometimes in the midst of silence,
We re-read old text messages just to reflect back on
the impact that special person has made in our lives!

"UNMASKED"

Just because someone paints a pretty picture, doesn't mean he or she is who they say. A lot of times they're hoping to be judged by perception rather than character!

"SUNKEN SHIPS"

They're gone but never forgotten
Abandoned out at sea
Some severely beaten by past storms
Others stuck in misery,
My heart would like to bring them ashore
rebuild their shattered dreams
Give them a renewed sense of hope
So they can gracefully sail again,
But in the midst of wanting to do good
I enjoy living drama-free
So instead of fighting with those other pirates
I've decided to just let them be!

"RELATIONSHIPS"

Relationships aren't easy. No one ever said they would be. People involved should know that every day isn't going to be rosy. They're going to be times when the two of you won't see eye to eye, pain might even come your way to test your commitment to each other. Just know the only way to get over that pain is to go through it. Once you've persevered and shown you have something worth fighting for, your heart would know you have something worth working with.

"LOVE"

To have loved at least once in your lifetime, says that you've experienced one of the greatest feelings in the world. Anyone that hasn't had that experience can never relate to the magnitude of such warmth!

"IF I HAD A SON..."

I would sit him down and tell him to include God in everything he does first and foremost. I would then remind him how important it is to get a good education. I would tell him there will come a time when he must make decisions in life all on his own, so he must learn to listen to his heart and trust his intuition. I would tell him to treat people with the utmost respect but don't let them walk over him. I would tell him under no circumstance should he hit a woman, because it would show a lack of respect for her and a sign of weakness in him as a man. If I had a son I would look him in his eyes and tell him of the many mistakes I've made, with hopes he won't make the same ones. I would speak to him about this imperfect world we live in and how he must learn to adapt and act accordingly. I would tell him no one is perfect and we all make mistakes, but it is very important to learn from each one. I would tell my son to always listen, because it would allow him to see things from different perspectives. I would remind him that all friends aren't necessarily his friend and how he'd be able to distinguish the difference in time of need. I would speak to him emphatically about morals and values. I would tell him to pray often because prayer changes things. I would tell my son to always have faith, because things won't always go his way, but with faith, he would have a reason to keep his head up. I would speak to my son about peer pressure and how insignificant material things are compared to the way he conducts himself in his every day walk of life. I would alarm him that he might be stereotyped, not because of who he is, but simply because of the color of his skin. I would tell him whatever he chooses to be in life, try and be the best at it. And when he finally asks me about love, I will say to him 'now is when you should listen to your heart!

"ALONE"

The morning dew has long dissipated
The sun has already started to set
Another day has almost come and gone
I haven't been wrongly accused about with whom I slept,
I don't mind having to explain my actions
I just don't like what happens when I do
Every time I lay my cards on the table
It seems my story gets misconstrued,
So now I cherish my days interacting with nature
Sipping coffee at the break of dawn
I no longer have to explain my every move
Ever since I chose to be alone!

"WITHOUT YOU"

The love songs I used to sing for you
Now just seem like shattered words
The white doves that followed us along the beaches
Now seem like ordinary birds,
The sunshine doesn't seem as bright anymore
The moonlight seem to have lost its glow
The ocean I once thought was so smooth and romantic
Now has an unusual flow,
The raindrops we used to listen to
No longer has that pleasant tone
Nothing seems to be what it used to
Since you've been gone
I've tried everything I could think of
But nothing is the same without you
I just want to enjoy the beautiful things in life again
The way you and I once used to.

"HURRICANE KAITLYN"

She came from the Midwest
Six years ago to be exact
She didn't pack heavy rain, gusty winds
Or anything like that
As a matter of fact
She was unusually laid back (for a hurricane)
She hung around
For a little more than a month
She discussed the things she likes (smiling)
And the type of career she wants,
I'd even looked at a few places where
I would treat her for lunch
But her time here was up
Before the first meal was ever launched,
Even though her stay was brief
The impact she had
left me 'soaked' and intrigued
I'd even wondered at times
Was she actually 'feeling me'
Or was I merely chosen
To help fulfill her fantasy!

"DREAMS OF SPAIN"

I keep having these dreams of being rich and famous
Living somewhere in Spain among total strangers,
Owning a couple of nightclubs in Barcelona
Investing my money and becoming a loner
I also dreamt of owning property
Outside of Madrid
Three to four acres
Just for my kids,
But every time I start to get that adrenaline rush
I get so upset
Because I find myself waking up
Realizing they were all just dreams
The scenarios kept changing
But it was always the same scene,
I'm really anxious to see this placed called Spain
Maybe there I'll find
Happiness, fortune and fame
And the best part about it
I might get to live my dream!

"SWIMMING WITH A SHARK"

She tried to warn me
Right from the start
She said she had a friend
That had stolen her heart,
even though I was warned
from the very beginning
I liked her so much
I kept right on swimming,
I know winning her over would be tough to do
So when she gave me an opening
I slipped right through,
Now that I'm in
The water seemed to have gotten deeper
I'm not so sure that she's a real keeper
I think she swims along
Plays her part
But she can't feel
Because she doesn't have a heart,
I've even thought about backing off
So maybe she could find the soulmate she'd lost.
But I also know that she really needs me
And swimming away from her isn't quite so easy,
But so often I ask myself
What role do I play

Am I just another 'fish'
Or am I standing in the way
I hate being confused from one day to the next
Feels like I'm tangled up
In a fisherman's net,
A part of me would like to leave
And get out of the dark
But there's the other side
That's madly in love with the shark!

"IT WON'T RAIN ALWAYS"

I have failed at more things
Than people would ever know
I've had my share of falls
Even though the scars no longer show
Despite the many things
That has gone awry
I still walk with my chin up
And my head held high,
Because I truly believe
It's only a matter of time
The rain will eventually stop
And I will get to cherish the sunshine!

"WORK IN PROGRESS"

My life isn't actually that interesting,
but I've got interesting things going on in my life!

"THE TRUTH"

Things won't always go as planned, nor will they happen in a timely fashion as we'd like. But every now and then something amazing will happen in our lives just to remind us who has total control.

"WHAT IF"

What if everything we've ever done in the dark
Was secretly recorded,
What if the culprits behind every rumor got prosecuted
For all the controversy they started,
What if 'walls could talk'
And told us everything that goes on behind closed doors,
Would we then try and keep our own houses clean
Or continue worrying about what you're doing in yours,
What if we could find out what folks say about us
By the flick of a light switch
Will we constantly overreact or
Let it slide off our backs as if
It were nothing more than a flake from an ice chip,
And what if Governor Romney didn't make
that stupid comment
About the 'other forty-seven' percent
We might have a leader that only cares
About half the people as our president,
Luckily, these thoughts came about
While my mind was still adrift
None of these things will ever happen
But it does scare me when I think..
what if!

"HMMM"

If anyone happens to run across my friend
Tell her I miss our conversations
And the cute text messages she used to send
I've tried everything from email to
Calling both her phones
Maybe she's going through something
And she'd just rather be left alone,
In any event I hope all is well
And she's just somewhere having fun
And didn't take the wrong turn in the wilderness
And a young 'cat' ended up getting her 'sprung'
And if that was the case
I wonder why she didn't keep her word
That no matter how good or bad things got
She would never kick a true friend to the 'curb,
Hmmm!

"PLAN"

Always have a plan. It is possible a pearl could miraculously fall into your hands by chance. But it is more likely to happen when you plan to go out and dig your own oysters. A plan is the blueprint for success!

"YOU"

I've sailed around the world twice
I've swam in the Caribbean seas
I've seen the sunset over many beaches
I've even dated celebrities,
I have shaken hands with former presidents
I've been taken to places I hardly knew
But nothing was ever so breathtaking
Than the day I first saw you,
Not only were you so beautiful
You spoke with such eloquence
In all my worldly travels
I haven't met anyone like you since
I've been asked many times
What had the most memorable view
I've seen a lot of fascinating things
But nothing as captivating as you.

"HAPPINESS"

Happiness can produce a smile so bright, not even a sea of clouds could overshadow its glow. Happiness also helps us to forget the harsh memories of our past. In my opinion, love is the only other feeling that compares. When one finds happiness, he or she then believes his purpose in life has also been defined!

"RUMORS"

They get started by certain people
that run their mouths without the facts
They take a story they've overheard
And begin to add to it or subtract,
Now the original story gets twisted
And the believers are agitated
Because the story they've just been told
Has been completely fabricated
Now everyone starts pointing fingers
Placing the blame here and there
When they all should've kept in mind
You can't believe everything you hear!

"SCORNED"

She constantly reminds me
she is a woman scorned
Her heart has been abused and severely torn
(but I want her nonetheless)
See the oddity of it all is
She thinks I'm attractive
She likes my qualities
But the matter of fact is (she's afraid to trust anyone)
So I thought I'd take her hand
And walk with her slowly
Give her an opportunity
To really get to know me
But every once in a while
I tend to get a little 'frisky'
I would whisper in her ear hoping
She'd lean over and kiss me (but she keeps her space)
I seriously think
She would like to cross the line
Let her hair down a little
To show me she's really trying
But instead of engaging
In anything that might leave her weak
She always end the night early
With a pleasant kiss on my cheek!

"LOSING"

You won't win in everything you do. So it is very important to remember not only to whom you lost, but also the reason!

"EYES WIDE SHUT"

Be careful of always reaching for stars. Because you might just miss your blessing by overlooking the 'diamond' you just walked over!

"MISTAKES"

I am not perfect by any stretch
I've made mistakes with many regrets
I have burnt bridges
I shouldn't have crossed
For which I had to pay a price
Four times what it actually cost
But I've since grown
And learned in the process
That living a perfect life is
Unheard of and farfetched
So I've taken those mistakes
And all the bridges I'd burned
try to build from it all
and just consider them 'lesson learned.

"SKELETONS"

Some folks believe it is good fortune when one door closes and another one opens. I, on the other hand, would rather make sure the house isn't haunted before I make that distinction.

"TIED TO A STRING"

I feel like I'm waist-deep in this jungle
Trapped in a cougar's den
I'm trying desperately to find an exit
But these two cats got me locked in,
The one to my left is awfully demanding
She likes her 'milk' three times a day
The one behind me is more laid back
She gets fed and goes about her way,
Needless to say I admire them both
Because they're different yet somewhat the same
But I realize I'm running on pure adrenaline
Trying to 'burn the candle' at both ends,
So one part of me would like to get out of this jungle
Walk away while I still can
But my 'wild side' likes the idea of having
Two cats so attached to one string.

"REMEMBERING WHERE I CAME FROM"

If I were to stumble upon success
Acquire fortune and fame
Become a songwriting sensation
and possess my very own airplane
(that would be so cool)
But it would all be for naught
If I suddenly start to change
Get caught up in a lifestyle
Of flamboyance and material things,
Lose sight of what's important
Like family and true friends
But I can promise this won't ever happen
Because I know exactly who I am
And how much of a disgrace it would be
If I forgot the road from which I came!

"ELIZA"

Sometimes out of the clear blue, she falls into my thoughts. I'm certain she doesn't even have a clue the impact she has. Maybe one day when I know she can reciprocate, I will show her the difference she's made. Meanwhile, I'll just cherish moments like this!

"KEEP IT TOGETHER"

When everything around you seem to be falling to pieces, and you can't hold it together no matter how hard you try.
Stop…use duct tape.

"FOCUSED"

When we're confident about who we are, and understand the direction in which we're headed, other people's perception of us matters not even a little!

"AT TIMES"

At times I still think about
How you swept me off my feet
I remember telling myself to be careful
I even tried to move cautiously,
I used to look past your bad habits
Because I wanted to work things out
I knew I wanted you to be my 'boo'
And I felt this without a doubt,
I remember asking you to marry me
Even gave you a diamond ring
At times I still get teary-eyed
When I reflect back on everything,
Even though it's been awhile
Oddly, I find myself waiting for your call
And wondering how things might've been
If I had not wanted it all!

"ALL OF ME"

I poured my heart out for you
And you knew it
You had me wrapped around your fingers
And you blew it,
It didn't matter how many women confronted me
It was always you I wanted standing
In front of me,
But you just wanted the thrill
Without commitment
Nothing else mattered
As long as you were getting it,
But I want you to listen for a moment
And keep still
I'm no longer interested in
Being your 'cheap thrill'
I want something more promising I can build on
Have something to show for
Once the thrill's gone
Maybe we'll meet again in my next life
Hopefully you'd want more than just a sex life
I can't say I won't miss you
But I have to move on
You shouldn't have a problem finding someone
To get your groove on

but as for me
I'm now looking for longevity
Not just someone
To go to bed with me
And when I find her
She'll be treated royally
Because I would be giving her all of me,
thoroughly.

"ALL OR NOTHING"

When I make up my mind to do something, I do it with a lot of passion and determination. Not just because I like being good, I like giving my all and best in whatever it is. I have this same exact approach towards love.

"A SOLDIER'S STORY"

I'm in the middle of an all-out war
With ten dysfunctional soldiers
I've got to keep one eye out for the enemy
The other one over my shoulders
Everyone in my platoon has an attitude
Each one feel that he should lead
I would like to honor their wishes
But none of them can tell the forest from the trees,
My colonel thinks this is humorous
Well I'm sick and tired of being laughed at
He keeps telling me things will get better
But I'm already way past that,
I'm sure they're going to court -marshal me
As soon as I throw my towel in
But I'd rather walk away with a peace of mind
Than continue butting heads with my own men.

"QUESTIONS"
(of a soldier)

Was that my last meal I just ate
Or does it even matter
Will I awake in the morning
And if so, what about the morning after,
Have I seen my family for the last time
I think not but it's been three years
I have all of these unanswered questions
But I'm not sure anyone's listening or cares,
I've been fighting in this crazy war for so long
I forgot my reason why
Maybe I'll get my answers when this is over
If I'm lucky and still alive
And let's say I'm still alive
Will I remember or will anyone remember me
Or will it just read 'he served his country well'
But now has schizophrenic tendencies!

"TRIBUTE TO MAYA ANGELOU"

Ms. Maya Angelou, I pray you are resting in peace. You set a standard in writing very few, if any, could compare. I took your idea of being somewhat of a loner until all of my goals were accomplished. You deserve the credit for setting such an example that works. Thank you so much for all you've done and the many lives you've touched along your journey. You are truly missed and I'm sure heaven could hardly wait to embrace your presence.

"SPEECHLESS"

You don't ever have to tell me that you love me, just continue to show me in ways words can't even begin to explain!

"PRIORITIZE"

Sometimes the thing we want most isn't necessarily a good thing for us. Often times a sign is revealed but our eyes are too blind to see. We must understand our needs should always be met far ahead of our desires!

"WILL YOU REMEMBER ME"

As I travel on this journey
Trying to broaden my horizons
To become a best-selling author
and songwriter on the rise' (will you remember me)
When you hear my lyrics
As they're being played on the radio
Will you remember me joking about
adding you in my video
or would you even smile
Or vaguely remember my name
Or would the memories by then
Have long faded in the wind
Or would you just smile and simply say
'I remember Him When'!

"REMEMBER"

Always remember that I adore you
And care about you tremendously
Even though your heart is elsewhere
I still think of you endlessly,
Remember how I pampered you
Even made sure you ate properly
I wouldn't have put forth the effort
If I didn't mean it wholeheartedly
So when I think back on everything
There's nothing I would've done differently
I just want the very best for you
And hope that you will remember me!

"IN TOO DEEP"

A lot of times we allow ourselves to get caught up in awkward situations, to the point where everything seem so vague and complex. But as soon as we take a few steps back, it is then we find clarity and understanding. Often times in order to move forward, we have to step back to get a better sense of direction!

"MY BAD"

I'm saddened and totally confused
Not knowing where she's gone
My days have all been cloud-filled
My nights hasn't been as warm,
Hopefully she's somewhere safe
Enjoying life and doing just fine
I hope she understands that I miss her
And think of her all the time,
Unfortunately, I don't think I will ever see her again
The thought alone is awfully sad
But I may as well be realistic
And just cherish the times we've had
If by chance I get lucky enough
To once again cross her path
I would tell her she was the ideal mate
I just didn't realize what I had.

"HOPE"

Hope is the inspiring force that allows us to believe that anything is possible. Hope allows us to have confidence even when doubt is staring us in the eye. No matter how dark and gloomy our day may appear, hope is the one thing that can lift our spirits and give us a sense of belief that tomorrow will be a brighter day!

"BITTER SWEET"

Be aware of your past mistakes, but don't dwell on them. A lot of times life will take us through the weeds just so we can appreciate the roses!

"GET @ ME"

I want you to understand
I'm more than worthy
There's more to me than writing songs and poetry,
See I'm quite a gentleman
And I know how to treat a woman right
I won't ever forget your birthday, your likes or dislikes,
See I'm ole school
I was raised differently from guys you've met
That's why I'm sure they are some things
I can surprise you with,
Like taking you on a cruise on a regular basis
Visiting different countries
Dining at exotic places,
Shopping at fine stores throughout Beverly Hills
We can go anywhere in the world
Depending on how you feel,
I'm not trying to impress you
I'm being honest and up front
If I was your 'boo'
You could have whatever you want,
See I want to be the one
To change your cold perception towards men
Patiently walk with you
Until you're ready to love again,

So if you feel what I'm saying and you would like to be happy
My points are well taken
You understand them exactly,
then don't waste another minute baby
Just come on and get at me.

"WHAT I WOULD DO"
(to please you)

First of all, I would take the time out
To find out…what makes you smile
I would also go that extra mile
Every once in a while
to show you I'm worthwhile.
I would take the memories from your horrid past
Throw them in the ocean
With killer sharks and crabs
(just to prove that your bad days are gone forever)
I would then take you with me
Back to the 'deep blue'
Show you that every wish you ever imagined
Can become true,
Your cloudy days would never again be gray
They'd be sky-blue
And everything you ever wanted in a man
Will be standing there before you!

"BEING DOWN"

Look at 'being down' as a positive.
In order to grow, you must first get buried!

"SKYE"

If I had my way,
I would appropriately rename you 'Iris'.
Simply because you are equally as beautiful as any 'Rose'
and definitely the 'apple of everyone's eyes'!

"WINNERS AND LOSERS"

Winners never use excuses in becoming who they are.
Whereas losers always has reasons why they aren't where
they should be!

"SO INTO HER"

She always walks away
Like a fool, I let her back in
Thinking that this time she might stay
But the same things keep happening
I'm so sick and tired of her
And her wicked naughtiness
I want to leave her alone so bad
But it's painful and obvious
I'm so into her that
I find myself getting accustom to
The silly game she plays each week
Really though it's nothing new
She's been gone for a minute now
But I know she'll be calling soon
She will have a brand new excuse
But really it's the same ole' tune
I'll listen to her story
And I'll have my share of doubt
But I'd rather have her to listen to
Than to go on without.

"UNTITLED"

When we decide on what we'd like to become,
and understand the path we should take to get there,
our blue-print for success is partly drawn.
Everything else is based on our determination.

"WHY I LOVE YOU"

I love you because
You're the other half that makes me whole
When we're apart
I feel helpless and out of control
When we're together
United as one
You make me feel I can reach out
And wrap my arms around the sun,
When I'm with you
I don't feel any sense of pressure
I am completely secure
And I feel very, very special
And if that isn't enough
As to why I love you so
I can easily write another page
But I'd hate to ruin the flow.

"HOLD MY HAND"

I just want to say 'thank you' lord
And I want you to know that I truly understand
How lost I would've been
If you were not holding my hand,
You've always filled my cup with everything
Whenever it ran empty
Through you I've had my share of opportunities in life
Because you provided aplenty,
You've always made me so happy
Whenever I was down or feeling 'blue'
You've always pointed me in the right direction
When I didn't have a clue,
So I just want to say thanks again
And I do understand how blessed I truly am
Even though you brought me through the toughest of times
I would like for you to continue holding my hand!

"I LISTENED"

You said I would never succeed
Nor did I possess what it took
You said I wasn't smart enough to comprehend
Much less write a book.
You said I wouldn't amount to anything
And my idea of success was all wrong
You said my dreams were too farfetched
And that I would never write a hit song,
Well I sat and listen as you criticized me
But I kept my head towards the sky
And prayed that when I become successful
You'd be able to look me in the eye,
I've since written over a thousand songs
At least half will be top hits
So I wonder has your perception of me
changed now that I'm filthy rich.

"A WHOLE LOT OF NOTHING"

I was told a painted picture is worth a thousand words.
So I'm painting this picture using my imagination and a few
adverbs. Here's the picture. I just said absolutely nothing.
So I'm wondering how this blank picture could still be
equivalent to that of a thousand words!

"I'VE GOT TO GET AWAY"

I'm sick and tired of the way I'm living
Hanging out all night with different women
I got to slow down so I can finally breathe
For once try and relax
So I can live my own dreams
I would like to 'chill out' on my balcony
And not worry about some 'thug'
Running in the back of me
Trying to carjack me for my black 'Benz'
Then turn around and try to sell it back
To my own friends
This life's got me 'fed up
All my friends talking to me
Telling me to keep my head up
I got to get away from this misery
It's so bad
I can't tell my friends from my enemies
I got to find a 'spot' in the countryside
And trade my fast cars and women in for buggy rides
I got to get away!

"A ROYAL FLOP"

A lot of queens say they want a king, but some of them aren't 'castle-ready'. They're still dealing with small 'jacks' and wild jokers and expecting royal treatment.

"TREASURE WHAT YOU HAVE"

When you have something you truly believe in, treat it in such a way that voices from a thousand critics couldn't change the way you feel!

"NOTHING"

If we take into account what we came with, and have a clear understanding of what we'll be leaving with, we might change our approach about what we're fighting for!

"EXPECTATIONS"

First of all, we should understand we cannot change adults. And nor should we try. We can either accept people the way they are or move on. Often times, we unfairly set expectations of others and when things don't go as planned, we feel he or she is a disappointment. When in all fairness, our expectations may have been too high and we placed the blame unfairly. The only sure way to not get disappointed is by not having any expectations.

"EFFORT"

We won't get everything we ask for every time. But that doesn't mean we shouldn't try every time at what we want!

"GET YOUR MIND RIGHT"

You won't ever find a perfect person. There isn't such a thing. However, you may meet people that will treat you right, do all the right things, and might even be a perfect fit for you. But because your mind is so contorted, you'd probably miss out on the opportunity. Simply because, according to you, they still weren't perfect enough!

"THE DIFFERENCE"

When you don't have ambition, a hill might seem like a mountain. But when you've got it, that hill seems like nothing more than a small bump in the road!

"TIME"

We should always value our time. Time is one of the things we will lose and never regain. Therefore, we should cherish each moment as if it's a gift. Because in many ways, that is exactly what time is…a gift!

"STILL WONDERING"

There was a time not long ago
I thought of her amongst all else
we settled being just friends
But I really wanted her for myself
There were times I sat at home
And literally cried until I fell asleep
Because I wanted so much more from her
But I realized that couldn't be,
Even though it's been a while
I still feel somewhat intrigued
Wondering how things might've been
If she didn't always have to leave!

"FOR ME"

It is not a priority of mine to try and fulfill your expectations of me. I will never try and be someone you want because I have my own goals and visions and more importantly, at the end of the day, I like to look in the mirror and feel proud, because I did things my way for me!

"A BLACK BEAMER'S RIDE"

Her boldness and unique style
Was the first thing that caught my eye,
I wasn't sure If I could afford her
But I wanted anxiously
To test her drive,
The first quarter-mile
She drove rugged and rough
As if she'd been sitting way too long
Or hadn't been driven as such
As I increased the speed a bit
Her engine started to 'purr'
As if she was saying 'drive me harder' baby
I'm built to handle the deep curves
Speeds got up so fast at times
It got really tough to breathe
If I didn't have my hands on the wheel
I could swear she was test-driving me,
But as the ride came to a close
I couldn't help but turn and grin
Because there was a sign on the dashboard that read
'Sir would you please drive me again'!

"SIMPLE MAN"

I'm thrilled with the small things in life
And I don't need a lot of notoriety
Anything that I do
I do it smooth and quietly
I'm not into the glamorous lifestyle
Or the high level of prestige
I don't have a lot of luxury cars
However, I can get whatever I need,
you won't find me asking for 'hand-outs'
Because I don't live beyond my means
I don't believe in a whole lot of excess
Just the bare necessities.

"IN THE LIME-LIGHT"

I place you on a pedestal so that when I finally reach my goal at the top, you will be close enough to dance with me among the stars!

"PROBLEMS"

These problems of late
Seem to be getting the best of me
My mind is so exhausted
I'm not sure it will catch up with the rest of me,
At times I feel like
I'm buried in quick-sand
Even my bad days seem
Like extended weekends
When I try to be rational
Some people seem to get mad at me
So I have to get lost sometimes
Just to maintain my sanity
my disappearing helps for a moment
But then reality kicks in
I know when I wake up in the morning
I'm faced with problems again!

"STRAIGHTEN UP"

Always walk with confidence and keep your head up.
If your head is always down, your blessings could pass
you by without you ever realizing!

"ANGEL"

She has a gorgeous smile
That is charming and bright
Her eyes are so beautiful
They seem to change colors in the sunlight,
She has long black hair
That reaches her chest,
I wrote a song about her once called
'The Angel I Kissed"
I remember her walking by
And how her looks always startled me
When she would ask 'how was I doing'
Her voice moved every part of me
I pray we meet again and
she remembers me as the 'stranger'
That found her absolutely adorable
and instantly nicknamed her 'angel!

"REMEMBERING THE HOOD"

I was constantly surrounded by
Chaos and mayhem
'crackheads' would ring my doorbell
Two and three o'clock in the am
Street walkers would pass through
On their nightly stroll
I remember 'drug-dealers' trying to convince teens
That 'hustlin' was more prominent than long-term goals,
And I definitely can't forget the girl on the corner
That called me rude and said I acted funny
Because I wouldn't buy the 'cookies' she was selling
Knowing it was just a cop-out for drug money
As I look back years later I realize
In some way we were all 'strugglin'
Some of us were just more determined
To make a better life that meant something
Even though I've gone on
I wouldn't trade my past life for nothing
And I would still lend a helping hand to those same folks
Because deep down
I'll always love em'!

"TO ME"

When I look at you, I see the true definition of beauty. It isn't just because of your model-like features or captivating smile, but more so because of your engaging personality that perfectly complements that smile. Which is why, to me, you are by far the most beautiful person I've ever met!

"ALL I HAVE"

I give 110 percent in everything I do. I take pride in whatever it is I'm doing. And I don't always win, but I do this so that if I should ever have to walk away from anything that I'd given my all, I would leave with a sense of contentment knowing I had nothing else left to give. This isn't to say that I gracefully accept failing, it is having an understanding that some things, no matter how badly I wanted, simply weren't meant to be!

"IMPERFECTLY PERFECT"

In a perfect world, I would write you pages and pages of love poems and send you different colored roses every single day, just so you'd have an idea how beautiful I think you are. But because we live in such an imperfect world, I can only give hints of the beautiful future that awaits you!

"ATTITUDE"

You can have all the talent in the world,
but if you've got the wrong attitude,
people with less talent will always take your place.

"HOW I KNOW"
(I am the one for you)

I know because when I'm with you
I feel a warm sense of security,
When we hold hands it seem
Time freezes, just so we get to cherish each minute longer.
When you kiss me
I'm reminded of how sweet and passionate
you've always been,
When I mention your name I'm told, my smile is
conspicuously brighter. When I'm in your arms,
I feel there's no other place in the world is as comfortable.
And what makes me so certain is,
whenever I look into your eyes
I always know with whom I'd like to spend
the rest of my life.

"ONE ON ONE"
(with the moon)

Moon, you and I have been talking on and off for quite some time now. It seems your glow tonight is as bright as it has been in weeks. I hate giving off this impression that I'm somewhat jealous, but I would like to know what brought about this beautiful radiance all of a sudden. I am curious to know also am I the only one, and if they're others, do they make you shine the way I do. I don't have a problem sharing you if I must, as long as I'm the only one that leave roses for you under the rainbow.

"I'M JUST A TEENAGER"

I'm just a teenager
I got my whole life ahead of me
I'm totally harmless
Yet the police say they're scared of me
(but I don't understand why)
See I'm too young to drive
So I take half-mile strolls
Sometimes I wear my 'hoody'
Simply because it's cold,
But my look is problematic
At least that's what I'm being told
But I don't see anyone bashing designers
for making these over-sized clothes
(but I get stereotyped for wearing them)
So talk to me America
Why am I being feared
I can't even walk a half-mile
Without having my hands raised in the air
And in case you haven't noticed
my life is always in jeopardy
police constantly chasing me
A hundred other obstacles ahead of me
So put yourself in my shoes for a moment
And picture life through my eyes

Why would I exert my energy trying to scare you
When I need every ounce of it to survive.

"ICING ON THE CAKE"

It is said that 'you can't have your cake and eat it too.
Well, I feel as long as everyone at the table is satisfied,
I don't see why not.

"TRIBUTE TO STEPHEN EDWARDS"

God took another friend on Wednesday
I guess it was his time
Wish I'd known he needed me
But I was much too blind,
So busy getting my own life in order
That I forgot to check on him
So now I'm left with a saddened heart
Because I've just lost a really good friend
However I know we'll meet again
And here's the very reason why
Because friends aren't supposed to walk away
without ever saying goodbye!

Rest in Peace Stephen!

"I WONDER"

So many of us are dying
It's getting hard for me to cope
Every other week I'm attending a funeral
Seems the world has given up on hope
Every day someone's being shot and killed
I wonder if this will soon end
For once can we finally put our guns aside
and learn to love again...
I wonder!

"WHY I WALK IN THE RAIN"

Most times I walk in the falling rain
searching for an answer that would ease my pain
to some I might look awkward or strange
But just because I'm different
Doesn't mean I'm insane,
I look to the sky
And pray to God for change
I always talk to him
Because he soothes my pain
And never do my prayers go in vain
I'm sure he knew what I was seeking
Long before it started to rain.
So the reason I choose
To walk in the falling rain
So I can leave my problems with God
And no one has to hear me complain.

"ON CHRISTMAS"

I plan to purchase the finest bottle of wine
Then prepare a gourmet dinner
Have the table elegantly set
With two candles in the center,
I will have rose petals throughout the hallway
Scented candles all along the stairs
A couple of logs burning in the fireplace
Just in case my queen appears
If I should happen to be so lucky
And she emerges from one of my dreams
I will gladly take her by the hand
then sing about what this all means
But if this Christmas is like all the others
Where she still isn't crossed off from my wish list
I'm going to wine and dine the night away
And pray she shows up after Christmas!

"WORD-PLAY"

Nowadays hunters have to be careful how they bait their prey.
Not all rabbits are deserving of the best karats.

"SLOW YOUR ROLL"

Not everything in life requires speed. If you concentrate on precision and consistency, you would always end up with a quality result.

"LOOSE ENDS"

They're what we end up with after realizing we couldn't have all of what we wanted. We were too afraid to let go, so we ended up settling for that small glimmer of hope that things might fall into place somehow. Loose ends is just another term used for anyone that leaves the door to their heart open for that special someone that still holds the key!

"GREENER PASTURES"

Just because the grass is greener,
doesn't mean it is always best.
Sometimes the pretty color
Is there to disguise the damaged roots!

"REFLECTIONS"

You become more appreciative of the sunshine
when you look back on the 'thunderstorms' in your lifetime!

"NOTHING COMPARES TO YOU"

You are always in the midst of my thoughts.
When you and I are apart,
I like to look up at the stars. Because it's the only thing I know
that replicates your scintillating beauty. Even then, I can't help
but notice, when the stars are at their brightest, they still don't
quite measure up to that incomparable glow you possess every
time you smile!

"TRIBUTE TO PRINCE"

Prince, I couldn't afford a 'Little Red Corvette'
back in the day, so instead I
bought a similar style 'Datsun 280ZX'
and had it painted red. I was so amazed at
how well you used metaphors, that I tried to emulate you by
writing a poem called
'A Black Beamer's Ride' in my very first book back in 2009'
(it became one of the most liked poems in the book).
And just to show how much of a fan I still am...
'If I should ever witness rain turn purple
Or live long enough to see doves crying'
I would say we will 'Adore' the man that sung this
'Until the end of time'!

"THOSE EYES"

She is uncertain where I'm leading her
Still her heart is very much intrigued
I can tell she would like to follow me
By the way she watches me when I leave
a part of me feel she's somewhat afraid
The other part thinks she's bracing her fall
Though her actions show she's very tentative
Her eyes are saying she wants it all.

"LEBRON"

In my opinion, LeBron James is the most dominating athlete in professional basketball. He wasn't always this way. He worked on his game relentlessly to become the superstar that he is. Despite his many outstanding accomplishments, he's also the most scrutinized player in his sport. He does so many great things for his community and kids all over the world and yet, they're some that hates him for one reason or another. I personally believe its jealousy. We live in a society where anytime someone is doing things in an unheard fashion, folks will always try to find negativity. So instead of appreciating James for what he's doing, folks unfairly compare him to arguably the greatest basketball player to ever play the game, Mr.Michael Jordan. Let us understand something. There will never be another Jordan, but the numbers LeBron James is putting up across the board has never been done, not even by Jordan himself. So I say let us appreciate what LeBron is doing right before our eyes, because we may not see this act again for many, many years to come.

"ROBBERY IN DISGUISE"

There are a few things about banks
That has always seem to bother me
The fees they charge for using my debit card
Is more like 'legalized robbery'
They can also take my deposit
Lend it to another for profit
Yet deny me when I ask for a loan
Explaining that though my credit score is sufficient
Doesn't guarantee me they would finance my home.
When I look at the overall picture of their wicked system
I realize the unjust right before me
But continue being trapped as one of the victims,
See, what they're doing is no different from Mr. Joe,
Who robbed them and got 'fifteen to life'
Their scheme is just better disguised
in the fine print of the policies they write.

"WILD DEUCES"

In a strange way, life is like a game of Poker. From the start, some of us are unhappy with the hand we were dealt. So we anxiously wait for a 'king' or 'queen' to come along and flush our hearts with hope and promises. But after a few 'shuffles', we realize this 'king' or 'queen' is actually a total 'jack', and those promises were nothing more than a 'bluff'. Unfortunately, we had to learn the hard way that not all pretty 'face-cards' are sure winners. And a lot of times, the 'deuces' we got in the beginning could have actually been a winner, but we didn't have the patience and ended up 'folding' too soon!

"WITH TEARS IN MY EYES"

I'm writing this with a heavy heart
And tears rolling down the side of my face
it hurts me that I have to live in a world
With so much hatred and prejudice amongst the human race.
It seems everyone is irritated
And their mindset have become reckless
Civilians are starting to retaliate against
The very officers our city hired to protect us,
It hurts me even more to see
The senselessness that happens soon after
People feel they have to post signs
And wear T-shirts to remind their
counterparts every life matter,
I'm sure God is watching this and saying
'My people have become more divided
instead of getting closer'
So I won't be a bit surprised
If he decides to wipe us all out
And just start over.

"YOURS TRULY"

I spend hours writing about our love,
because I know they'll never be another love like ours!

"TO EACH HIS OWN"

It is okay to be different. You look at the stars in amazement at how far away and beautiful they are. I look at what I must do to become one.

"THIS ISN'T POETRY"

Fellas, if you've got a good lady at home, treat her right. Always be a gentleman. Open and close her door when she enters and exits. Make her smile often. Try to remember all those dates pertaining her. Treat her out to places she's never gone before. Buy her flowers on occasions. When the two of you aren't seeing eye to eye, treat her out to a great movie. Most times, by the time the movie ends, she will forget why she was so mad in the first place. Never go to bed upset. Try to resolve any issues the two of you had before going to bed. Don't ever be too proud to say 'I'm sorry"(its only two words, but they go a long way). If she has had a bad day, cook her dinner. Make her feel her entire day wasn't so bad. This isn' t poetry or a how-to-love guide. These are simply quality things that men have gotten away from. Keep in mind, she may forget those sweet things you told her in the beginning, she might even forget some of the places you took her, but never in a hundred years will she forget the gentlemanly manner inwhich she was treated.

"OUT OF MY HANDS"

I've been fighting with a bit of uncertainty lately
Unsure how far this songwriting and poetry will take me
I feel if my audiobook doesn't sell
Or none of my books reach the 'top ten'
Part of me will start believing
What the naysayers were saying back then,
But somehow my heart still has confidence
And believe there's a bright spot for me
That I would one day be mentioned
In the same breath with Shakespeare or Jay-Z,
But even if this doesn't happen
I'm staying true to my first plan
To do everything in my power to succeed
Then leave the rest in God's hands!

ABOUT THE AUTHOR

I was born in Savannah Georgia and raised on beautiful Hilton Head Island, South Carolina by my aunt and uncle, the late Maggie and John Holmes Jr. I feel proud and blessed to have grown up in such a lovely and beautiful environment. However, I am most proud of my three daughters, twins Shakera and Shanera Snyder and Alexis Johnson, who are all grown up and off to college. I have written three other books, 'A Part of Me' vol.1, 'If I Had A Son', vol.2, and 'The Mindset of A Mockingbird'. Without question, I consider this 'Collector's Edition' my best project thus far. This book has several intriguing short stories along with some of my work from my previous books that I had revised. When I decided years ago that I wanted to become an author, I had no idea my fan base would extend as far away as Argentina, Brazil, India, Barbados, Canada, Germany, Switzerland, Belize, Bosnia, Japan, and of course here throughout the United States. It goes to show that having a strong belief, determination, and a good work ethic, anything is possible.

By Bernard Snyder